Every Question Will Be Asked

HAROLD COPLAN

Stanley A. Edlavitch, PhD, MA

editor

Paperback ISBN-13: 978-1-946469-81-6
Hardcover ISBN-13: 978-1-946469-85-4

ShelteringTree.Earth, LLC Publishing
PO Box 973, Eagle Lake, FL 33839

ShelteringTreeMedia.com

DEDICATION

For my father

~ Harold Coplan

For my wife Carol of 35 years; Harold's daughter and the most spiritual person I have ever known, who maintained her faith during years of chronic illness.

~ Stanley Edlavitch

FOREWORD

This poem sat untouched in my late father-in-law, Harold Coplan's papers for more than 35 years. He was an educated Kohein, and the poem reflects a knowledge of Jewish searching for God and mysticism and reflections on his and our relationship to God. He challenges the meaning of our existence and our relationship to the universe and how we perceive creation and God. In this poem, he shares a difficult personal search to understand our existence. The questions he raises are universal and are not restricted to people who believe or are affiliated with any specific religion.

I would like to thank Larry Edlavitch, Seth Edlavitch and Adam Edlavitch for their support in preparing this document.

I

We are weak beings, easily frightened, afraid of our existence.
Through our weakness the world trembles and quakes. Life
becomes empty; the world becomes empty.

We are alone.
We or I? I am alone.

I feel no kinship with the world; yet I exist.
Existence is my mother, my father; existence is my God.

I exist as a rock exists.
I am as important as the world.
I am as insignificant as the world.
I am like a rock.

I am like a rock?
No.
I am less than a rock.
I think.

If being had meaning, the meaning would be a joke.
Or does the joke exist… without laughter?

Or perhaps man is the joke, and rocks that cannot think are
laughing all the time.

Man is the joke; he thinks.
He thinks thoughts so perishable, so finite.
And thoughts are the essence of his death.

But rocks cannot think.
They can only laugh at man and at existence.
They laugh eternally; they laugh silently.
Through infinite days and infinite worlds, rocks laugh.

II

And man is alone.

Would that he could be alone, that he could hide from things, from any thing.

Would that he could hide from someone.

Would that man could hide.

But man is alone, contemplating life and death, existence or lack of existence.

He cannot hide, cannot know if he can hide.

He may live or die, or live and die, or neither live nor die.

Who cares?

In time, no one cares.

In time, there is no time.

The illusion at the passing day will disappear, and illusion, too,

will disappear.

In time, the infinite will shatter finite worlds and die herself

an infinite death.

Call it life.

Neither term describes a death of life; a life of death.

Today is illusion.

No time, no space - illusion.

Today exists

Until tomorrow.

III

Faith exists in paradox.
Paradox exists in doubt.
But faith strengthens doubt,
While doubt weakens faith.

The strongest faith proclaims, "I do not believe."
Then faith negates itself.

Still bereft of the possibility of a warming faith,
    we plod along a mystical path toward God or godliness,
    not sure if such a path exists.

"Plod along?" We do not know the destination of where we are, or
where we have been.

"Plod along a mystical path toward God

    or godliness."

How little the name matters.

There is no succor in the name of the search.

There is no solace, no confirmation because we search.

IV

We are like rats in a maze.

We think – like them.

We run – like them.

We are confused – like rats.

We search for God - or godliness- like rats that search for food.

There is a difference.

The rat will find his food and eat.

His maze is real.

At least we know his maze exists or did exist.

We know nothing about our search save that we search or try to search.

We plod and so we plod.

V

To our search we may ascribe the name of God

    although He may be absent from our searchings.

To our search we may ascribe the name of God

    although we may find that He is absent from our searchings.

    although we may never find that He is absent from our

    searchings.

That we search proves nothing.

We may never find God nor ourselves.

VI

Today I begin my journey.

I shall step forward; I shall step backward.

No.
Today, I am beginning my journey.
I shall not move at all.

My path is mystery.
There is no path, just direction and I shall not move save in the direction of my journey.

I shall not move at all.

VII

God calls me.

VIII

Nothing holy has happened.
Nothing has happened to make us holy
    save death and dying
    and the dying man's thoughts of death.

But death is not holy
    just sufficiently profane to be considered holy.

And death is too frequent to be holy.
Death is too much a part of life to be holy.

Perhaps a saint has passed this way – to make us holy.

No, no saints have passed this way.
And if they did, they would not matter.
Saints are not of this world
even if there is no other world.

No, no saints have passed this way.

And if they did, they would not matter.

People do not tolerate saints or saintliness.

IX

God calls me, I think.
But God calls you
    and you
and almost no one listens
    or
God calls only you and me, I think.

Who am I that I should taste divinity?

In the name of pride, in the name of humility, I reject God's call.

I must search alone for myself by myself without God.

I must search alone to find God; to find there is no God; to find
nothing at all.

X

The World calls me.

The World?
This world is a desert, or this world is a jungle.
If a desert, our mouths are parched dry; we cannot speak.
The heat of the day confuses us.
If the world is a desert, we shall die in the heat of the day.

This world is a jungle.
If a jungle, it teems with too much life; life confusing life.
The jungle is wet and alive: too alive.
If demons exist, God is alive among them in the jungle.
We shall not live out the confusing of the day in the jungle.

XI

Perhaps God exists because Hell exists.

XII

So, the Midrash says: *When the prophet Malachi died, God stopped talking.*

God stopped talking?   Does He talk? How? He has no mouth.
And when He goes to sleep, does He close His eyes?
When we pray, can we hold his hand?

We have insufficient signs to know what God does not do.
We have insufficient signs to know what God does do.

God held our hands when we did not know that God has no hands
to hold.
People cannot hold God's hands.

XIII

There was a time when man prayed to God.

Now man prays before God.

He cannot find God.

God is hiding

Or man is lost.

He is out there, up there, transcendent, immanent.

He is the parts the make the whole; and greater than the whole.

Nothing exists without His presence:

      nothing exists where He is present.

His word is our existence.

His word is the residue of His being.

He is paradox within paradox and no paradox at all.

To deny Him is to admit the possibility He exists.

To proclaim that possibility is to admit He might not exist.

Man's faith is founded upon words like these.

But belief and nonbelief are deeper than words.

And words can damage belief, all belief.

Empty words can freeze a soul

      and a keep a thinking soul from death

      can keep a soul from, thinking death.

XIV

We are dying.

We are dying men.
> We must speak as dying men speak.
> We must hear what dying men hear.

Our words, our thoughts must burn, must boil, as constant prayer to God.

Must be scalded to stand before a living God.

Because that is how dying men stand before a loving God.

Still empty words may freeze a soul
> may freeze a soul from death

and empty words can make the finite real.
And man, constantly challenged to speak, may ask about the weather.

Some will listen.

No one will care.

XV

And man, when talking about the weather,
     may only be talking to himself even when talking to other
men about the weather
     may only be talking to himself.

And man may speak about the weather in his impatient search to
find his soul
     to find his God.

And man may speak about the weather to find the day is chilly.
He knows that. So what?

He does not care about the weather.
Man cares about himself
He speaks into a mirror - to another man – to find himself.

Man would do better if he would look at the other

If he would look

    silently

    at the other man.

If only he would see that other man.

XVI

In silence there is revelation
        sometimes.
Sometimes in silence there is nothing except the silence.

That, too, can be a revelation.

By silence
At least by silence a man can make himself small.

And when in silence he finds he is not there
        then man has found himself.

XVII

Or man may pray to God
Who will be silent about the weather.

Or man can pray to God - to find God.
Man can pray to God and find that almost all is God.
But God is more than all.

Man could find that almost all is God
Then man would find himself.

XVIII

Prayer is difficult for people who know that they are praying.

Think on this.

A most solemn prayer will be-in time-defiled by God.
In time man will lift his prayer above his God
        will lift his prayer and make a substitute for God.

And prayer to God may destroy the man who prayed one time to
find his God.

HAROLD COPLAN

XIX

Entropy

The world destroys itself -

Man destroys himself and dies.

XX

Blame God.

Man could pray if God did not cause the entropy of the prayer.
Man could pray if God did not cause that entropy of worlds.

XXI

Blame man.

Who can reject a world of entropy and live.
Who can accept a life too short to be affected by the entropy of
God.

In time

      man may live

      may find his God

      may find himself.

In too much time

      man will die destroyed.

XXII

Man, to live, must remain like sand – irreducible - like sand
Must say: "I am like sand- and alone."

Sand, swallowed by the infinite shore
Anonymous, alone
Sand that cannot grow because it cannot think
      never realizing the power of the surf and the shore
      never realizing that quantity defiles.

Never realizing that quantity is relative - not real
That quantity makes the relative real
Makes big, big and small, small when both – the big and the small
Do not exist.

And God does not exist with big or small.

XXIII

So man defiles God's holy word
Man, becoming holy, defiles the word of God.

The priest arose to meet his God
He stood too tall when he tried to be small.

A humble man turns proud because he spoke to God.

A humble man was humble when he spoke with God

He sinned
His humility was a sin
Remaining humble was a sin.

HAROLD COPLAN

XXIV

From dialogue with God, no man remains the man he was
From words to God, no man remains the man he was

No man can find himself in God
No man can feign to share the world with God
He needs nothing, must search for nothing, and realize nothing to realize God.

XXV

Ultimately, one question remained.
There was a time
        when every phrase and every word
        cried meaning or lack of meaning
        when every act and every moment
        pleaded understanding
        demanding misunderstanding
But
        Ultimately
        ultimately, one question remained
        reminded us of possibilities of a world with half a meaning
                of hell.

We must survive with meaning
We could survive no meaning

We torture through half meaning.

XXVI

In the beginning, God created the heavens and the earth
Infinite and finite kissed.
For a moment, God acted in time
But infinity surrounded moment
There was no moment except that moment
Nothing was finite until that moment
And then
> God, for a moment, gave up infinity.

For a moment, God was not God
> or He was God
By the power of that moment.
Or He was God, who showed by finite action
> the infinite capacity of His being of His nonbeing.

One question remained when infinite and finite kissed.

One question about a God who stopped being God and was thus God.

One question remained to a finite creature

Who saw God deny His own infinity

      through creation.

One question remained for a finite creature

Who, by his existence, denied creation

Who, by his existence, denied infinity.

Who, because of his existence, could not find God.

One question remained and remains still.

XXVII

Until the search
God was never absent.
He was a fact, an idol

Smashed by the search
    absent in the search.

.

XXVIII

Knowledge becomes weakened by knowledge.

Soon there is no knowledge

    just words

    relatively important

    meaningless.

Meaningless all the same.

Soon there is no search.

XXIX

And the way of the search is not to search at all.

XXX

A paradox.

There is a God.
We must lose him.
There is life
We must lose it.

There is meaning
We must deny it
Before we search.

The way of the search is not to search at all.

And the absence of a paradox.

We must learn from the dead.

We must not search at all.

XXXI

One final word

There are questions which must be asked
Questions which must be answered.

There are questions which must be asked
Which cannot be answered
Which cannot be answered.

In time, every question will be asked.

In time, every question will be asked.

ABOUT THE POET

Harold Coplan (Copey)

Copey was a war-hero with superb people and management skills. He was born in 1922 and enlisted in the army Air Corps. During World War II, he was a bombardier and flew in 34 missions over Western Europe. He was recalled to active duty during the Korean conflict. His plane was shot down in 1952. He was declared missing in action and held by the Koreans and Chinese as a prisoner for eight months under severe conditions. He was considered a hero who, as senior officer, was offered release but refused release without his crew.

Following his return to the US, he continued business management education and became the base operations officer at several major Air Force bases. Copey was devoted to his family and was known as the peacemaker in both his professional and personal lives. His intelligence, education and knowledge of Jewish thoughts and mysticism show throughout this poem

Though Copey was a Kohein (descendent of Priestly class) and raised as an Orthodox Jew, he switched to Reform Judaism later in life. He did continue to perform the rituals of the Kohein when called upon and celebrated the major Jewish holidays in Reform tradition. Due to his untimely death during surgery, we do not know if the questions raised in this challenging thought-provoking poem were a result of this long incarceration and torture by the Koreans and Chinese.

ABOUT THE EDITOR

Stanley A. Edlavitch, PhD, MA.

Professor Edlavitch is an epidemiologist with a long successful career in academia, the pharmaceutical industry, government, consulting, and the non-profit world. He has published more than sixty scientific articles, several book chapters and one book related to public health.

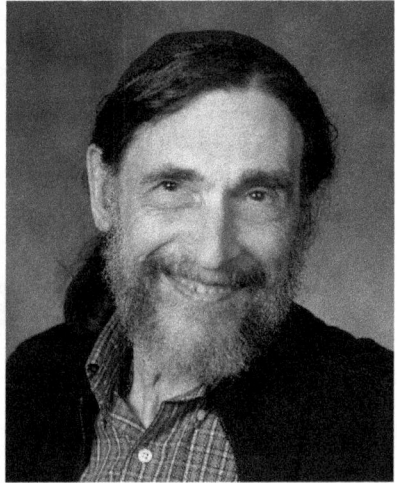

The past few years, he has been meeting with clergy in several countries, learning about their insights about God and the role and practice of formal religion. In a recent visit to seven Orthodox Clergy, he asked for guidance on where to read or study answers to four basic questions. Hundreds, if not thousands of articles have been written on each. The four questions were:

Why believe in God?

If one believes in God, why follow a religion?

If religion is important, why follow a specific religion?

And finally, how can we explain and accept the behaviors of those professing and preaching ethics and morality from various pulpits, who do not behave accordingly?

Though this poem does not address all of those issues, it

was fascinating to find that my late father-in-law had been grappling with some of the same issues and it is an honor to help bring the poem to print.

DISCUSSION GUIDE FOR SMALL GROUPS, CLASSES, OR INDIVIDUAL REFLECTION

1. Why do you think Coplan named this poem *Confessions*?

2. How did you react to his suggestion that the rocks and sand may be laughing at man?

3. Given he was brought up as an Orthodox Jew and was a Kohein, did you feel he was confirming belief in God or questioning the bases of his upbringing and expected behavior? Please explain.

4. Coplan was a hero and for 11 months was a tortured prisoner of war.   In what ways does the poem's questioning his/our presence in the universe and relationship to God make even more sense knowing he had this experience?

5. Did you think his conclusion that all questions will be asked is optimistic or pessimistic?   How so?

6. What reasons might he have had to not mention religion in the poem?   How would you put religion in the context of this poem?

7. Do you feel that Coplan asked his questions and answered them?   Which questions did he seem not to answer?

8. What do you think he meant when he said the God was never absent until we searched for him?

9.   *Pantheism* - the belief that God and the universe are identical, meaning that everything in the universe is a part of God or is God.

Animism -   the doctrine that every natural thing in the universe has a (individual) soul. (no universal God)

Atheism - A lack of belief in God or Gods.

Chabad teaches that God's presence is immanent in all creation, while at the same time God is fundamentally beyond and separate from the created world. This is a key difference from pantheism, which merges God and creation into a singular identity.

Do you interpret *Confession* as closer to expressing beliefs of pantheism, animism, atheism or closer to Chabad's interpretation of God? Why?

10.   How do you interpret Coplan's statement that today is an illusion and man is alone? What experiences in your life support that statement?

11.   What do you think of his thought that perhaps God exists because hell exists? Give real-world examples to support this. Then give real-world examples to deny this.

12.   Do you agree or disagree with that there was a time man prayed to God, now man prays before God and we cannot find God.   Why?

SHELTERING TREE
●
EARTH PUBLISHING

Shelteringtreemedia.com

We are an exclusive publishing house. We specialize in uplifting, inspirational, and positive adult, juvenile and young adult, fiction and nonfiction, including poetry, native histories and spiritual paths, sermons, lectio divina, and pastoral and rabbinical resources in English, and other languages.

www.ingramcontent.com/pod-product-compliance
Lightning Source LLC
Chambersburg PA
CBHW060422050426
42449CB00009B/2079